LOVE THE EARTH

Understanding climate change, speaking up for solutions, and living an earth-friendly life

by Mel Hammond

illustrated by Monique Dong

★ American Girl®

Editorial Development: Mel Hammond, Barbara Stretchberry

Art Direction & Design: Jessica Rogers

Production: Caryl Boyer, Cynthia Stiles, Jodi Knueppel

Illustrations: Monique Dong

Special thanks: Professor Daniel J. Vimont, Bridget Edmonds

Even though instructions have been tested and results from testing were incorporated into this book, all recommendations and suggestions are made without any guarantees on the part of American Girl. Because of differing tools, materials, ingredients, conditions, and individual skills, the publisher disclaims liability for any injuries, losses, or other damages that may result from using the information in this book. Not all craft materials are tested to the same standards as toy products.

americangirl.com/service

PLANT TREES

BE THE CHANGE!

Solar panels

Reduce

Reuse

Recycle

EARTH

Dear Reader,

You love the earth—it's your home, after all. Maybe you've heard that the earth's climate is changing, but you don't know why that's a bad thing. Or maybe you know a lot about climate change already, and you're ready to raise your voice to make a difference. Wherever you are on your earth-lover's journey, you're on the right track.

This book explains the basics of climate change and how you can use your unique skills to help stop it. With quizzes, crafts, party ideas, and a science experiment, this book proves that fighting climate change doesn't have to be scary—it can be a lot of fun! And best of all, *anyone* can do it. Ready to get started?

Your friends at American Girl

LOVE the EARTH

Say No to PLASTIC

eco

GREEN

CONTENTS

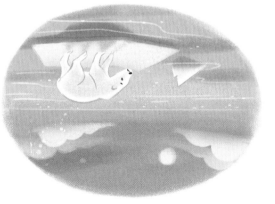

Live a Climate-Friendly Life . . . 52

THE EARTH NEEDS OUR LOVE

Our planet gives us so much:

Air to breathe

Water to drink

Food to
eat

Beautiful forests,
mountains, deserts,
prairies, and rivers
to explore

Wonderful
people to meet
and spend
time with

What do you
love about
our planet?

The Planet Is Getting Warmer

It's called **climate change,** and it affects us all in different ways.

Before humans started driving cars, flying in airplanes, and making products in factories, the planet was about 1.7 degrees Fahrenheit cooler than it is today. That might not sound like a big difference. But a small rise in temperature across the whole planet is a *huge* deal.

Here are some of the ways a 1.7-degree increase has changed the earth so far:

• **Ice near the North and South Poles is melting.** Cold-weather animals can't find enough food. Ground that usually stays frozen year-round (called *permafrost*) is melting and becoming unstable, which causes homes and roads to fall down. The problem especially affects *Indigenous communities*—groups who have lived in an area for thousands of years.

• Melting glaciers and warming oceans are **raising sea levels.** People who live near a coast or on islands are losing their communities to floods and storm surges.

Hurricanes and other storms are becoming stronger. These storms cause damage and flooding and can make it hard for people to get food, clean water, and shelter.

• The air is becoming hotter and drier in many places, which makes dangerous **droughts, wildfires, and heat waves** more common.

Plants and animals are struggling to survive in warmer temperatures. Some animals migrate to new areas. Many plants and animals die.

You might already notice some of these changes happening outside your window, or you might only hear about them on the news. Luckily, there are things each of us can do to help. The first step is learning about the problem, so reading this book is a great start.

Earth-Lover's Notebook

As you learn more about climate change, you might find it helpful to keep all your notes, ideas, questions, inspiring quotes, research, and doodles in one place.

You will need:

-  An adult to help you
- 15 sheets of paper that have been printed on one side (Check around the house or in last year's school folders.)
- A 2-hole punch
- Cardboard from an old shipping box or shoe box

- A pencil
- Scissors
- String, yarn, or ribbon
- Decorations like stickers, bottle caps, magazine clippings, and colorful tape
- Craft glue

1.

Fold one piece of paper in half, with the blank side facing out. Use the hole punch to add two holes to the paper, on the open (non-folded) side.

2.

Repeat for all 15 sheets of paper.

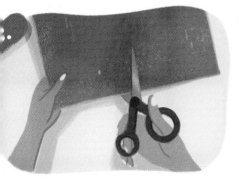

Cut two rectangles from the cardboard, inches wide and 9 inches tall. These are he front and back covers.

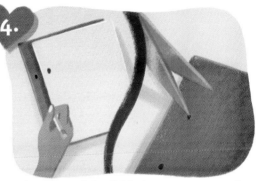

Place one of the folded papers on top of the front cover. Use the pencil to mark where each hole is. Do the same for the back cover. Ask an adult to cut a small circle at each mark with the tip of the scissors.

Cut two pieces of string, yarn, or ribbon, each about a foot long.

Stack the pages, front cover, and back cover together. Carefully push the string through each set of holes and tie a tight bow with a double knot.

Brighten up the front cover with whatever decorations you like.

Keep an eye out for this symbol throughout this book. It means there's something special to write in your notebook!

Life in the Greenhouse

The earth has a blanket of air around it called the **atmosphere**. Having an atmosphere is the reason we can breathe. (Thanks, atmosphere!) But this layer of air has another job, too: keeping our planet the right temperature for us to live. Here's how it works:

Energy from the sun passes through our atmosphere and heats up the earth. Most of that energy radiates back into space, but **greenhouse gases** trap some of that heat like a blanket. This is called the **greenhouse effect**, and it helps keep the planet a comfortable temperature.

The Greenhouse Effect

Atmosphere

The problem is that humans have been adding *too much* greenhouse gas to the atmosphere—much more than exists naturally. These extra gases are trapping more heat, causing the earth to warm up.

Wait. Why is it so cold today?

Some days it might feel as cold as ever outside your door. That's because you're feeling weather, not climate. What's the difference?

Weather is what's going on in the atmosphere at a certain time, in a certain place. Is it hot or cold? Is it rainy, snowy, foggy, or icy? Is the sun shining, or are there clouds in the sky? Weather can change from one minute to the next.

Climate is what weather looks like over a long period of time. For example, if you live in Phoenix, Arizona, your climate is warmer than it is in New York City, even if the weather is cold some days. When scientists look across the entire world, they see that the climate has been slowly but surely warming up.

MON TUES WED THUR FRI

1970   2020

Ask an adult: How has the environment changed since you were a kid? Write down their answer.

The Fossil Fuel Blues

Most of these extra greenhouse gases come from burning **fossil fuels.** Humans have been burning *a lot* of them lately.

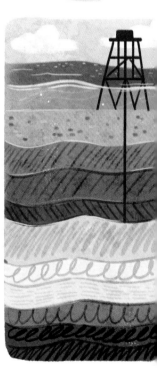

What are fossil fuels?

Millions of years ago, plants died, decayed, and were slowly buried under the ocean floor.

Eventually, time and pressure transformed them into high-energy materials such as coal, oil, and natural gas.

Humans can take these materials out of the ground and use them for fuel. *Fossil* fuel—get it?

We use fossil fuels to power our cars, make electricity for our homes, fuel our airplanes, create plastics, and power the factories that create clothes, packaging, food, and toys. If you live in the United States, about 96% of the products you use every day were made with fossil fuels.

The problem is that fossil fuels release a gas called *carbon dioxide* (or CO_2) when we burn them. CO_2 is the main greenhouse gas that's causing the climate to warm up.

Say CO2 like this: *SEE-OH-TOO.*

Humans breathe out CO2—does that mean that breathing contributes to climate change? No. Breathing is part of the earth's natural cycle. When we burn fossil fuels, extra CO2 is released into the air that the earth isn't used to handling. So breathe easy!

One way scientists know that CO_2 makes the climate warmer is by examining data across many years.

2016 was the hottest year on record (58.7°F)

Global Temperature and CO2

As humans put more CO_2 into the atmosphere, the temperature rises.

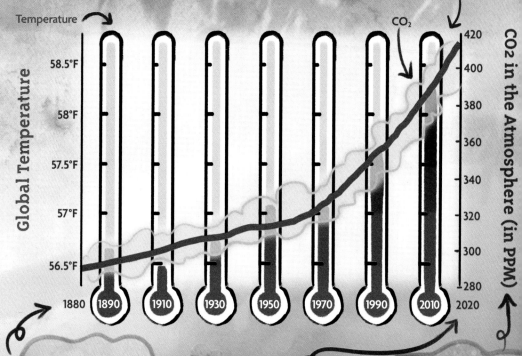

Back in 1880, CO2 levels were just starting to rise. North America and Europe had been using fossil fuels to power factories and steamships for about 100 years.

Today, CO2 levels and global temperatures are the highest they've ever been. And we're still burning more fossil fuels than ever.

Parts per million (PPM is a unit scientists us to measure how muc CO2 is in the atmosphe 300 PPM means that i million particles of ai 300 of them are CO2

Lexine D. is standing up for the Gwich'in way of life in Alaska

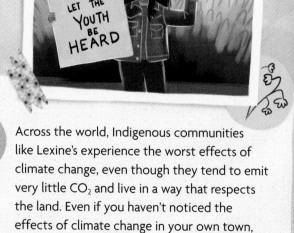

leven-year-old Lexine loves fishing and unting in Arctic Alaska. Her people, the wich'in, have fished and hunted in that ea for thousands of years. But temperaures in far-north areas like Alaska are rising vice as fast as anywhere else.

see changes all around me, in our rivers nd our lakes," Lexine says. When she went mping last year, dead birds lay on the round and fish floated in lakes and rivers. ildfires caused so much smoke that she uldn't see even a few feet ahead of her.

 make things worse, fossil fuel compaes are threatening to drill for oil in one f the most sacred parts of the Arctic ational Wildlife Refuge, where 40,000 orcupine caribou calves are born every ear. The Gwich'in consider these animals cred and rely on them for food. Drilling ere would hurt the caribou, which would en hurt the Gwich'in.

To fight back, Lexine and fifteen other young people are suing the state of Alaska. They argue that the government is putting their health, safety, and traditions at risk by encouraging companies to drill for oil. Lexine is using her voice and making people all over the world pay attention!

LET THE
YOUTH
BE
HEARD

Across the world, Indigenous communities like Lexine's experience the worst effects of climate change, even though they tend to emit very little CO_2 and live in a way that respects the land. Even if you haven't noticed the effects of climate change in your own town, pay attention to girls like Lexine who have.

CO2 in Action

That CO_2 in the air doesn't just warm up the atmosphere—it soaks into our oceans, too. That's bad news for the plants and animals that live there, because CO_2 makes the oceans more acidic.

Warmer, more acidic water is causing colorful coral reefs to turn white and die. Animals like crabs, oysters, and scallops have a harder time growing strong shells in acidic water. And animals higher in the food chain—including humans—can't find as much food in the ocean as they used to.

You can watch what CO_2 does to water in your own kitchen. This experiment uses red cabbage juice, which naturally changes color when it becomes more acidic. That makes it great for showing what's going on in your water!

To simulate the extra CO_2 in ocean water, this experiment uses sparkling water. Fizzy water is actually just water with added CO_2. That's what the bubbles are, and it's why some people call it *carbonated* water.

See for Yourself

You will need:

-  An adult to help you
- ¼ head of red cabbage
- A pot
- Water
- Clear fizzy drink, such as seltzer or lemon-lime soda
- A strainer
- 2 clear jars or cups

1.

With an adult's help, chop the cabbage into chunks. Place in the pot with enough water to cover. Bring to a boil and remove from the stove.

Pour the cabbage water through a strainer into two clear jars. The juice should be bluish purple.

3.

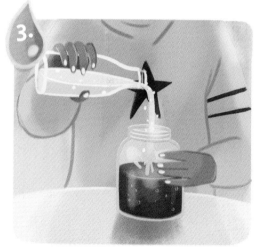

Add several splashes of fizzy water to one jar. The juice should turn bright pink, which means that the water is acidic! Compare it to the other jar to see how much the color has changed.

Just as the CO_2 in the fizzy water makes the cabbage water more acidic (and pink), the CO_2 soaking into the ocean is making the water more acidic. And the plants and animals that live in that water are suffering.

Cool It!

We can slow and even stop climate change, but we have to act fast.

Scientists agree that instead of using fossil fuels, we should start using *clean energy* (also called *renewable energy*) as soon as possible. Clean energy is power that doesn't run out and doesn't pollute the earth.

Solar energy

The sun delivers more power to earth in one hour than the entire world uses in a year. We just need to capture it! Solar panels sit on roofs and in open areas, transforming sunlight into electricity.

Wind power

Wind turbines stand in breezy areas such as open fields. The wind moves the blades of the turbines, and that spinning power turns into electricity. One wind turbine can create enough energy to power about 1,000 homes!

Hydropower

Water creates energy as it flows downstream through streams and rivers. We can use dams with underwater turbines to convert that motion into electricity. About seven percent of the electricity in the United States comes from hydropower.

Geothermal power

Deep under the ground, the earth is filled with hot, molten rock. We can drill holes miles down into the earth and use that heat to spin turbines and make electricity. If you've ever seen a video of a volcano erupting, that's actually geothermal energy in action!

What about natural gas?

Natural gas is a fossil fuel that many people use for heating and cooking. Some energy companies call natural gas "clean" because it doesn't add as much CO_2 to the atmosphere as coal and oil do. But it's not clean. Natural gas still contributes to climate change, it's not renewable, and collecting it from the earth can be harmful to workers and people who live nearby.

Trees, Please!

Trees are better than any other plant at keeping CO_2 out of the atmosphere because they can store it in their dense trunks, branches, and roots. The more healthy forests we have, the better.

Trees are also important for essentials like houses and books. And unlike fossil fuels, trees are a resource that grows back. When companies harvest trees responsibly, forests can stay balanced and healthy.

Many companies don't treat trees with respect. They cut down entire forests to make room for animal farms, crops, mines, roads, and buildings. Sometimes they use fire to clear what's left, which adds more CO_2 to the atmosphere.

Look for a Forest Stewardship Council (FSC) label on paper products to know that they use wood from a sustainable forest.

Since 1990, forests have been disappearing from the earth at a rate equal to

1,000
football fields
every single hour.

Scientists agree that harvesting trees responsibly, protecting existing forests, and planting new trees are important ways to protect the planet.

Turn Fear into Fuel

Climate change can be scary, but those fears can fire you up to make a change.

In your Earth-Lover's Notebook, make a list of some things that scare you about climate change. Writing your fears down can make them less scary. They can also help you figure out what you care about most.

My climate change fears:

- A flood or storm will hurt my home.

- Droughts will make it harder for farmers to grow enough food.

- I won't be able to swim in my favorite lake because of pollution and toxic algae.

- A wildfire will happen nearby and give my sister an asthma attack.

- Climate chang[e] will damage national park[s] before I get the chance to visit them.

- There won't be any fish left in my favorite fishing river.

- Whales and elephants (m[y] favorite anim[als] will go extin[ct]

Asthma

ASTHMA ATTACK

Choose a topic on your list that you'd like to learn more about first. (You can research another one later.)

Next, research! Here are some ideas:

Read books, articles, or news stories about asthma.

NEWS

ASTHMA TODAY

- Talk to someone involved in air pollution activism.

ACT NOW

THERE is NO PLANet B!

March

- Chat with friends or teachers at school about air pollution—maybe your science teacher has more information.

Listen to leaders standing up for the issue of air quality.

We need clean air in the future. Our children, their children need a home, and this planet is the only one we've got.
—U.S. Representative Ilhan Omar

Advice from Ms. Baez:
- Watch asthma documentary
- Research how racial inequality affects asthma in communities of color

Make a list of everything you learn:

- About 1 in 10 kids has asthma. Climate change is making asthma more common.

- Black and Latinx communities bear the biggest air pollution burden, which leads to more asthma. To change that, we to need fight for clean air and good health care in communities of color.

- Warmer temperatures and polluted air mean more ground-level ozone, an invisible gas that irritates your lungs. It's especially bad in big cities on sunny days.

- Kids are more likely to get asthma if they live in an area with lots of traffic. Better public transportation, bike lanes, and sidewalks are great ways for cities to reduce traffic.

- Having lots of trees and plants in your neighborhood helps keep the air clean and healthy.

Researching the issue you're passionate about can lead to amazing discoveries. Maybe you'll find an organization dedicated to keeping air clean for kids. Maybe you'll connect with a local leader hosting an air-quality fundraiser. There's so much to uncover!

A wildfire fired up Alexandria V. to change the world.

When Alexandria was 13, she was visiting family in California when a terrible wildfire broke out. Even though she was almost 100 miles away, the smoke was thick enough to give her an asthma attack. "My chest started to get prickly," she says. "I felt like needles were pinching my chest." She had to return home to New York City to escape the smoke.

We want world leaders to hold polluters accountable.

After some research, Alexandria learned that climate change causes wildfires to become more intense and frequent. So she started protesting. Every Friday, she sat outside the United Nations building to urge world leaders to take action against climate change.

Alexandria's activism became bigger than she ever dreamed. She created a climate-strike organization, Earth Uprising, and became one of the youngest organizers of the 2019 global climate strikes. She joined fifteen other young people in a lawsuit against five of the biggest polluting countries in the world. She even gave a speech at the United Nations—the same building she protested outside of every Friday!

"It's time to make our voices even louder, and spark a course correction for all of humanity."
—Alexandria V.

27

SPEAK UP FOR SOLUTIONS

Climate change is a big problem. But people all over the world are working together to create even bigger solutions. Are you ready to join them?

What Kind of Earth Lover Are You?

Help solve climate change *your* way.

1. Which school project sounds like the most fun?

   a. Interviewing your state representative about her plans to reduce your state's use of fossil fuels

   b. Inventing a phone charger that gets its power from the sun

   c. Working with other students to plant trees in a park

   d. Creating a video about how climate change is affecting people in your city

2. You and your BFF are having a sleepover this weekend. What activity do you plan

   a. Making *Vote for Me!* buttons for your upcoming run for class president

   b. Creating a hilarious machine that launches sauce, cheese, and toppings onto a pizza crust

   c. Puddle-stomping in the woods

   d. Decorating a BFF bulletin board with your favorite pictures.

• Climate change has caused a lot more rain in your town, and now many neighborhoods are at risk of flooding. You . . .

a. call the mayor's office to ask for more plants and less concrete in your city, which could help absorb floodwater in the future.

b. design an app that helps families find safe, free places to stay if they need to leave their homes during a flood.

c. help put together emergency kits with food, water, and blankets and pass them out to families in flood-prone neighborhoods.

d. create a digital poster with flood safety tips and ask your parents to share it online.

4. At school, you learn that reducing food waste and eating less meat are great ways to slow down climate change. You . . .

a. talk to your principal about adding more veggie-based meals to the cafeteria menu.

b. invent a reusable wrapping that students can use to keep their uneaten food fresh for later.

c. volunteer to work in your school's new garden, which will help provide fresh veggies for cafeteria meals.

d. give a presentation for a class project about why food waste matters and how to prevent it.

5. You've been selected for the school dance planning committee! What job do you choose?

a. Student representative. You'll meet with adults to help pick the theme, music, and snacks for the event.

b. Sound squad. You'll set up the stereo system so that kids can hear the music from every corner of the room.

c. Decoration team. You'll help put up streamers and banners on the day of the dance.

d. Hype girl. You'll make posters, send out emails, and speak on the morning announcements to let everyone know about the event.

6. Your U.S. senator says he opposes wind energy for your state because it would be too expensive. You . . .

a. organize a protest in your town.

b. calculate how much money windmill would save over 20 years and share results with him.

c. Volunteer at a walkathon to raise money for a new wind energy proje

d. Make a collage of a windmill using bottle caps, plastic containers, and single-use utensils, and enter your work in an art show.

Answers

Mostly a's

 Loud and proud leader. When you speak, people listen. You have big ideas, and you're ready to let people know about them. You'd enjoy leading a protest, talking to your elected officials, and helping others get involved with a cause. Maybe you'll even run for office one day!

Mostly b's

Savvy scientist. Asking questions, staying curious, and solving problems are what you do best. You love to tinker with technology and create clever solutions to everyday problems. Look for climate change issues that require analyzing numbers or inventing new tools. And when you fail, remember that scientists learn from their mistakes. Keep trying!

Mostly c's

Hands-on helper. You love to roll up your sleeves and get the job done, even if it means getting dirty. You enjoy working with others on projects, so consider volunteering at a community garden or joining a climate change club. Even when a job takes hard work, you know how to make it fun!

Mostly d's

 Eager educator. You love spreading the word about climate change so that as many people as possible can understand the issue. Whether you're hanging posters, giving presentations, filming videos, or creating works of art, you love to help people learn what's going on in the world. Remember— you don't have to know everything about the issue before you jump in. You can start now!

Which kind of earth lover are you? Are you more than one type? Solving climate change will take a lot of different strengths and interests, so everyone has something to contribute.

Real Girls, Real Change

Jocelyn C., Danny C., and Sofia R. helped their school cafeteria switch to reusable spoons and forks.

 When eleven-year-old Jocelyn learned that her cafeteria was throwing away 1,000 plastic spoons and forks every day, she talked to the principal to try to change things. The principal had a proposition for her: If Jocelyn and her fifth-grade class could teach other students about reducing waste and train them to keep reusable utensils out of the trash, the school would make the switch.

 Danny and Sofia joined the effort, and the three classmates started creating posters and lesson plans about reducing plastic waste. Then they taug their lessons to every class in the school, in both English and Spanish! They adjusted thei message to suit kids of different ages so that everyone could understand.

 When the cafeteria switched to reusable utensils, every fifth-grade volunteered to monitor the garbag cans and remind students to put spoons anc forks in the right places. The new program worked great!

Reshma K. invented a tool to help predict the future.

Thirteen-year-old Reshma lives in San Jose, California, where climate change is making wildfires more common. She researched what tools scientists currently use to predict fires and found out they were slow and expensive. She thought that if a tool could predict a fire early enough, people would have time to evacuate and firefighters could keep the flames under control more easily.

 Reshma thought of an idea to use information like humidity, wind speed, soil moisture, day of the week and month, and temperature to predict when a fire was likely to break out. She created a computer model, tested it, and kept improving it.

For a contest, Reshma made a video to educate people about wildfires and explain how her project could help. She won the chance to work with a mentor, who helped make her project even better. She ended up taking home the Improving Lives Award!

Girls on Strike

Kids all over the world are marching, demonstrating, and skipping school to get the attention of leaders. They're shouting the message: We need action on climate change now!

Protesting is a great way to let elected leaders know what you want them to do, even if you're not old enough to vote. If it sounds like something you might want to do, be sure to:

- Always get permission from a parent.

- Invite others! Protests are more powerful (and fun) with friends.

- During the event, stay with an adult chaperone at all times. Choose a meeting place in case you get separated.

- Bring snacks! Standing up for the earth works up an appetite.

- If you have to leave school, let your teach know ahead of time. Always make up the work you miss.

- Use markers and poster board to make a sign. Write a message with bold, easy-to-read lettering.

- Prepare for the weather. Bring an umbrell or poncho, plus an extra sweatshirt and a pair of sunglasses.

Havana C. E. is little but loud!

[N]ine-year-old **Havana** loves to protest. [In] first grade, she participated in a national [s]chool walkout against gun violence by her-[s]elf. Then she started marching for climate [c]hange and even speaking at rallies!

"[I] am used to grown-ups underestimating [m]e," she said during a speech in Washing-[t]on, D.C. "And right now, grown-ups are [u]nderestimating the climate crisis, too."

> One girl is powerful, but a movement of girls is unstoppable.

Havana has traveled all over the world, and she's noticed that Black and Brown girls face the most climate challenges. That's why she's extra loud about educating girls, which helps them build stronger communities and cope with events like droughts, floods, and food shortages.

Listen Up, Leaders

Even before you can vote, you can make a difference in government. Here are some ways to let your leaders know that things need to change:

• Write a letter or email

• Make a phone call

• Speak at a city council meeting

• Visit a leader's office in person

• Create a video about your issue and send it to a leader

• Text a family member who can help spread the word

Choose the method that works best for you. If talking on the phone is scary, try writing an email. If you don't enjoy writing, meeting with someone in person might be fun.

Pro Persuader Tip:
Make sure you reach out to the right person. Talking to your mayor might be great way to get a new community garde started in your town. But she wouldn't be able to do much about getting rid o tax breaks for fossil fuel companies. You need to reach out to your U.S. senator or representative for that.

Here's an example of a letter or email you might write to your city council members, who make the rules for your town:

Introduce yourself and say how old you are.

Explain the problem and how it affects you.

Dear Newport City Council,

My name is Maya, I'm nine years old, and I live in the Eastgate neighborhood. I'm writing to let you know that my family lives in a food desert, which means we don't have a grocery store in our neighborhood. To buy fresh food, we have to take a 45-minute bus ride. My family ends up eating a lot of food from corner shops and fast-food restaurants nearby, because we don't have time to go to the grocery store.

About 9,000 people in Newport live in food deserts like I do. This is unhealthy for us, and it's unhealthy for the planet. Fast food comes with a lot of paper and plastic we have to throw away, and processed food comes from factories that pump a lot of greenhouse gases into the atmosphere. I want to help protect the planet, but most days I have to either eat this food or go hungry.

If you can, include a fact that helps prove your point.

I'm asking you to say yes to a new policy that would bring grocery stores to neighborhoods like mine. A new grocery store would help my neighbors and me eat healthier and slow down climate change. It will also help make sure we can still afford food as climate change gets worse and processed food becomes more expensive. If you wait to act, the problem will keep getting worse.

Explain what you want the reader to do and how it will help.

Thank you for considering my idea. I hope you'll support this policy to eliminate food deserts in our city.

Sincerely,

Maya Williams

End by saying thank you.

Invent, Create, and Innovate

To protect the earth from climate change, we need solutions that haven't even been invented yet. You don't have to have a white coat and a fancy lab to get started—everyone can be an inventor. Here's how:

1. **Think.** In your Earth-Lover's Notebook, make a list of the problems you've noticed at home, at school, in your town, on the news, or online.

Problems:

- A lot of trucks drive down my road every day, and it makes the air smoggy.

- People keep leaving the door to our apartment complex open . . . even when the AC is on!

- When it's sunny, the playground equipment at school gets so hot that we can't touch it.

- Some people in my city don't have clean water to drink.

> There's tons of gum stuck to the sidewalk—and I stepped in some today!!

2. **Pick.** Choose one idea to tackle first. Look for problems close to home that matter to you. If you're new to inventing, start small.

3. **Research.** Why does the problem exist? Has anyone tried to solve it yet? If so, can you improve on that idea, or does the problem need a brand-new solution?

- Gum is made of artificial rubber, which comes from fossil fuels.

- Gum takes hundreds of years to decompose! Plus, most gum packaging isn't recyclable.

- Lots of gum ends up in the ocean, and it makes fish sick.

- People used to chew gum made from sap from certain trees.

- Someone invented a way to turn gum into rubber toys.

Imagine. Write or draw ten possible solutions for the problem. Don't worry yet about how you'll make it happen—even a ridiculous idea could inspire a realistic solution.

A robot that scrapes gum off the sidewalk

A sidewalk that plays an embarrassing song if you spit your gum on it

A special recycling bin that turns gum into rubber balls

• An earth-friendly gum that washes away in the rain and comes in recyclable packaging

A gum that tastes good forever, so you never have to spit it out

Narrow down. Pick just one idea you think would work best. You can always come back to a different one later.

Make. Create a *prototype* (a small, first-try version of your invention). If your idea needs expensive materials, try building your prototype with clay or cardboard first. If your idea is for an app or computer program, use a mock-up tool on a computer to make a pretend version. It doesn't have to work perfectly yet—it's just your first try.

7. Test. Try out your model and write down how it goes. What worked? What needs improvement?

8. Improve. Fine-tune your model and try again until it works the way you want.

> **Earth Gum**
> • Chicle gum base
> • Powdered sugar
> • Corn syrup
> • Food coloring
> • Bowl
> • Mason jar
>
> • Flavorings: cinnamon sticks, vanilla extract, mint leaves, ~~lemon~~ 😖
>
> ♥ how to make gum break down faster?

9. Share. If your model works, let people know about it! With a parent, look for contests for kid inventors online, submit your project to a science fair, or pitch your idea to a company. You can also look for an expert to help you improve your invention, like a cousin who's studying engineering.

Caroline C. invented a new kind of train that can run without fossil fuels.

Thirteen-year-old Caroline lives in New York City, where pollution from cars, trucks, and buses is a huge problem. After some research, she learned that traffic pollution is the number one contributor to climate change in the world and that it causes health problems such as asthma. Trains are one of the most earth-friendly ways to help people move around, but most trains still run on fossil fuels.

Caroline imagined a train that runs on magnets and clean energy instead of fossil fuels. She used a computer program to plan out how the train might work. Then she built a prototype with a model train track, plastic tubing, an air compressor, magnets, solar panels, and a battery.

"My design can be less expensive and more efficient than current train technology," she says. "It eliminates the need for a diesel engine or an electric motor, which makes the train lighter, so it can move faster."

She entered her idea in a contest for young scientists and got to work with a mentor to help her improve the idea. She ended up winning second place!

Idea Sparks

Here are some suggestions to get your creative juices flowing.

plant a lot of trees quickly?

move around town without fossil fuels?

warn kids with asthma when air pollution is high?

convince picky eaters to love veggie-based meals?

encourage people to make climate-friendly actions throughout the day?

get more kids to volunteer for eco-friendly projects?

alert the public when leaders are considering new climate change laws?

help kids continue their education, even after a natural disaster?

put food waste to good use?

protect families that live near toxic facilities from polluted soil and water?

help floodwater drain into the ground quickly?

keep sea creatures from eating plastic?

Get Your Hands Dirty

 If you're a hands-on helper, you love working with others and seeing the results of your work. Here are some jobs to try!

- Join a group planting trees on city streets.

- Clean up trash and recyclables from a beach.

- Help with a wildlife survey to track animals that live in your area and understand the challenges they face.

- Collect school supplies for girls around the world. (Scientists say that educating girls is one of the most important ways to slow climate change.)

- Help with setup and cleanup for a climate change protest.

- Volunteer for a trail-building day to help more people connect with nature.

- Research rain gardens and build one in your yard.

- Help build houses for people experiencing homelessness. (Houses help everyone stay safe during natural disasters and severe weather caused by climate change.)

Olivia W. isn't afraid to roll up her sleeves.

Native grasses to plant:
-Panicum virgatum
-Sorghastrum nutans

Thirteen-year-old Olivia noticed that her favorite beach was shrinking, and invasive weeds were taking over. She interviewed leaders familiar with the beach to learn about what solutions people had already tried. She also researched what kind of plants originally grew in that area. With permission, she started growing grasses from seeds in her house. Six weeks later, she recruited other young people to help her plant the seedlings on the beach. To keep the grasses safe, she put caution tape and signs around the area and watered them for months.

Seeds ♥

"It was an incredible experience to see the grasses go from tiny and brown to fuller green grasses thriving in the sand," Olivia says.

Join the Club

Loving the earth is better with friends!

Check with your teacher to see if your school already has a climate change club. If not, here's how to start one:

1. Research your school's rules for starting a club. What forms do you need? How often is your club allowed to meet, and where? Who is allowed to be the adult sponsor?

New Club Registration	
Club name:	The Earthlings
Meeting days:	Every Tuesday, during lunch
Teacher sponsor:	Ms. Lopez

2. Find other kids who share your passion and ask them to join. You might be able to put up posters and send out an email to reach more kids.

3. At your first meeting, play a get-to-know-you game to help everyone feel welcome. Talk about what kind of problems your club wants to tackle.

 Plan your first project. Decide on a day and time and gather all the supplies you'll need.

 5. Work together to complete the project!

6. Celebrate your work. Share what you did in a school newsletter or on the morning announcements. Then devote a meeting to eating special treats, playing games, and giving each other kudos for a job well done.

Spread the Word

Educating people about climate change is one of the most important steps for solving the problem.

- Talk to your family about a climate change story you saw on the news.

- Do a school project about climate change.

- Make art about climate change.

- Make a video about how climate change is affecting people's lives in your state.

Shruthi and Caroline made picture books about climate change.

Seventh-graders Shruthi and Caroline created picture books to teach younger students about climate change. "First we got information from websites," Shruthi says. "Then we had to figure out how to put it in a way that young kids could understand."

Shruthi's group wrote about John Muir, an environmentalist who helped create many national parks in the United States. Caroline's group made a book about a plastic straw named Samuel who goes on a journey from a trash can to the ocean.

The Adventures of John Muir

Samuel's Adventures

"We were kind of nervous reading the books to the kids," Caroline says. "But they seemed to enjoy it. Our book was about a big problem, but the kids stayed focused."

"It scared me, how climate change was coming so quickly. I wanted to see what I could do to get the word out."
—Caroline

"If you care about climate change, talk about it every chance you get to inform more people."
—Shruthi

Convincing a Skeptic

 Some people still don't believe in climate change. They want everyone to keep using coal, oil, and natural gas so companies can keep making money.

Studies show that kids are better than anyone else at convincing their parents that climate change is real. Showing that it's important to you helps!

- Ask respectful questions to find out what they believe and why. People like being listened to.

- Find something you both care about, like hotter temperatures in your town. Let them know how those changes make you feel and ask what they think about them.

- Keep your voice firm but calm. Kindness works much better than yelling.

Remember that beach you used to take us to, Grandpa? We can barely play there anymore because the ocean is so high now.

Hmm. You're right. That beach has changed a lot.

attling off facts probably won't change someone's mind. But it's important for you to know
e evidence so you feel confident when you talk to climate skeptics. And if the person
ou're talking to says something false, calmly state what you know to be true.

If they say . . .

Remember . . .

"There's not enough evidence."

→ 97% of scientists agree that humans are changing the climate.

"It's still cold where I live!"

→ A changing climate affects each area of the world differently. Some places have hotter temperatures, some have more rain, and some even have colder winters.

"Temperatures are changing on their own—humans don't have anything to do with it."

→ The earth has gone through cooler and warmer periods. What's different this time is that humans are emitting more greenhouse gases than ever before. That's making the climate get warmer over decades instead of millions of years.

"The research is fake and people on the news are lying."

→ That's what fossil fuel companies want people to think. Tobacco companies confused people in the same way so they could keep selling cigarettes, even though scientists knew they were deadly.

u probably won't change the person's mind today. It's hard for people to
mit when they're wrong about something, and they'll need some time to
nk about things on their own. But the conversation will plant a seed in
eir mind that will keep growing until eventually they'll understand.

LIVE A CLIMATE-FRIENDLY LIFE

You can show your love for the earth every day.

HHF
HAPPY HARV
FARM

How Big Is Your Carbon Footprint?

Your *carbon footprint* is the total amount of greenhouse gases you add to the atmosphere just by living your daily life. Everyone has one—even the most earth-friendly people you know. Knowing what yours looks like can help you make smart choices every day and throughout your life.

Circle one answer for each question below. Then use a pencil or crayon to color in the corresponding number of squares in the footprint.

How do you get to school?	Walk or bike (0 squares)	Bus, subway, or ferry (1 square)	Car (3 squares)
How many trips have you taken in an airplane this year?	Zero (0 squares)	One (2 squares)	Two or more (4 squares)
How often do you eat meat?	Never (0 squares)	Once or twice a week (1 square)	About every day (2 squares)
How often do you get brand-new clothes?	Rarely—I wear hand-me-downs and shop at thrift stores (1 square)	Often—I wear a mix of new and used clothes (2 squares)	Always—Used clothes? Ick! (3 squares)
How many hours a day do you use screens?	Less than two (1 square)	Two to five (2 squares)	More than five (3 squares)
Does your family recycle and compost table scraps?	Always! (1 square)	We usually recycle, but food scraps go in the trash (2 squares)	No, we don't recycle or compost (3 squares)
How do you stay clean?	5-minute showers (1 square)	10-minute showers (2 squares)	Baths (3 squares)
How often do you get fast food or eat at restaurants?	Rarely—we almost always eat home-cooked food (1 square)	About once a week (2 squares)	Twice or more each week (3 squares)
Which of these homes sounds most like yours?	An apartment in a building with other apartments (1 square)	A house you share with another family, or a mobile home (2 squares)	A house for just you and your family (3 squares)

Color in the green
footprint first. If you
fill that one, move
on to the yellow, and
then the red.

Answers

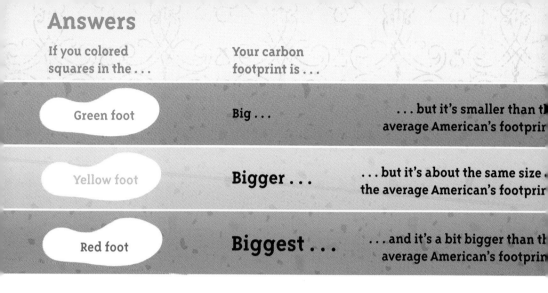

If you colored squares in the . . .	Your carbon footprint is . . .	
Green foot	Big . . .	. . . but it's smaller than the average American's footprint
Yellow foot	**Bigger . . .**	. . . but it's about the same size as the average American's footprint
Red foot	**Biggest . . .**	. . . and it's a bit bigger than the average American's footprint

If you live in the United States, it's pretty much guaranteed that your carbon footprint is bigger than most other people's in the world.

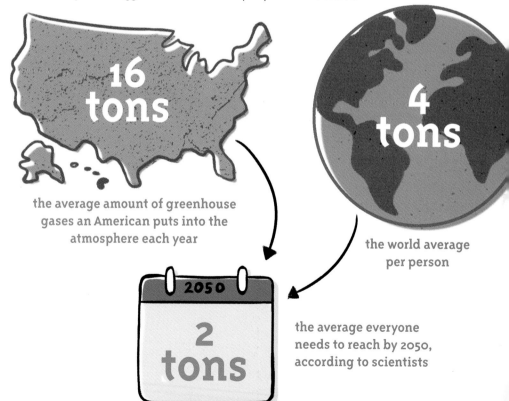

16 tons

the average amount of greenhouse gases an American puts into the atmosphere each year

4 tons

the world average per person

2050

2 tons

the average everyone needs to reach by 2050, according to scientists

o these facts mean you should feel guilty and ashamed? No. That doesn't do any good. stead, we can learn from each other, so that everyone can work together to do better. ere are some great things other countries have done!

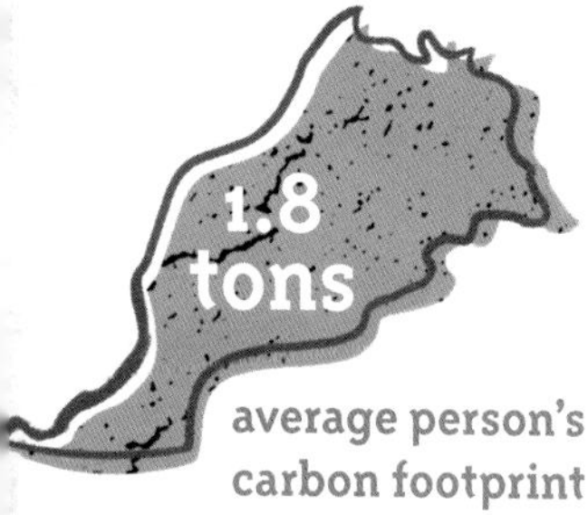
1.8
tons
average person's
carbon footprint

Morocco built the largest farm of solar panels in the world—as big as 3,500 football fields.

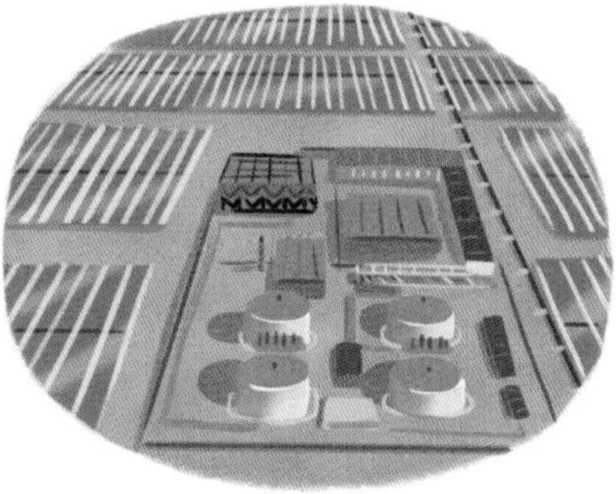

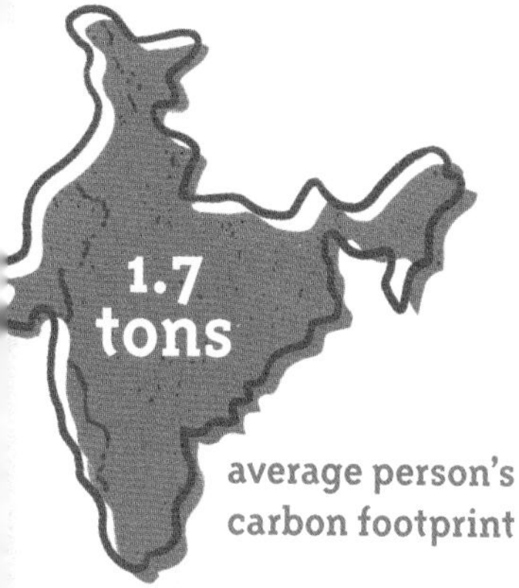
1.7
tons
average person's
carbon footprint

India invests more money in clean energy than in fossil fuels.

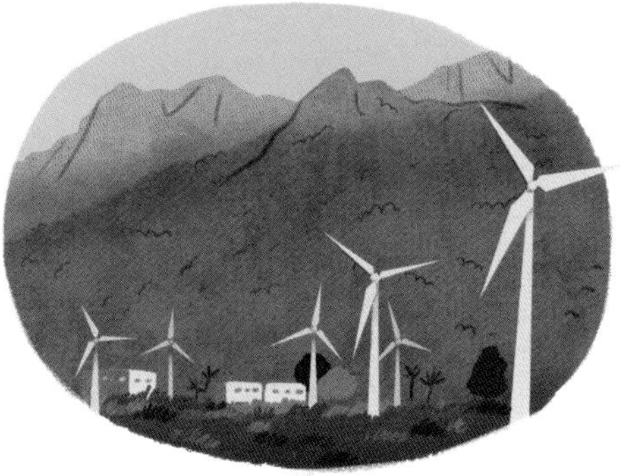

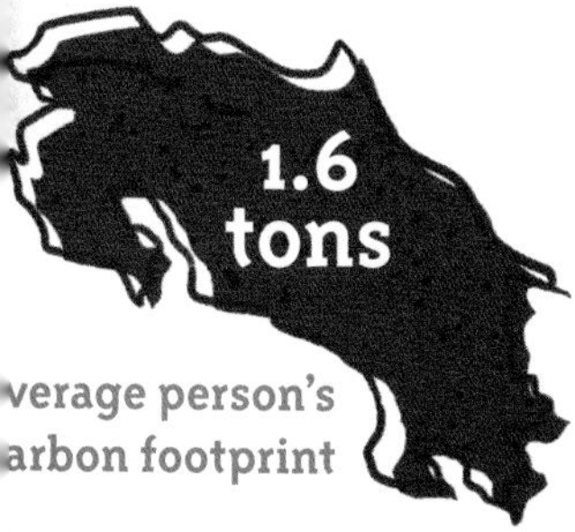
1.6
tons
verage person's
arbon footprint

Costa Rica gets most of its energy from hydropower, and it no longer allows companies to take oil out of the ground.

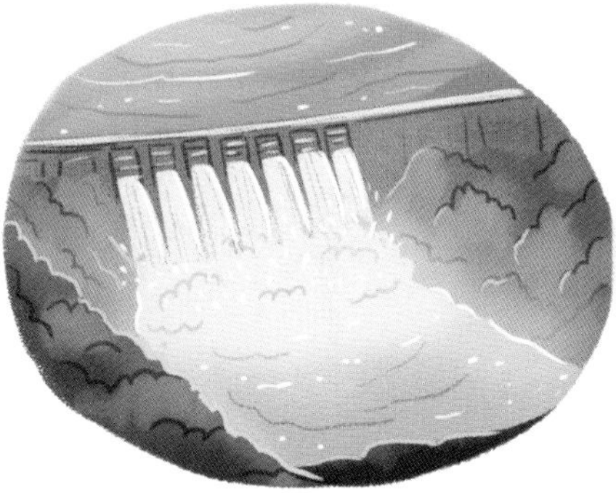

this section, you'll learn to change the habits you can (like recycling), stay informed about e things you can't (like the house you live in), and start imagining a world where our daily oices help the planet instead of hurt it.

Use Less

One reason Americans' carbon footprints are big is that we use more *stuff* than folks in other countries.

When factories make *stuff*—clothes, pens, frozen pizzas, plastic bags, soccer balls, kazoos, cell phones, fruit snacks, karaoke machines, nail polish, Fourth of July decorations—they also make greenhouse gases. And after a while, a lot of that *stuff* ends up in the dump, where it breaks down and releases more greenhouse gases.

CO_2

CO_2

CO_2

CO_2

CO_2

Some stuff we need.

Some stuff we don't need, but it gives us a little boost of happiness.

Some stuff we're better off leaving at the store:

In your Earth-Lover's Notebook, write down the stuff you've used so far today. Try to remember all of it—from the toothpaste you brushed your teeth with this morning, to the controller you used for your favorite video game, to the marshmallow-flavored lip gloss you just rediscovered at the bottom of your backpack. Then divide everything into three lists:

Stuff I really needed:

Toothbrush/toothpaste
- Comb
- Clothes, shoes

Notebooks, pencils, backpack
- Books

Stuff I could live without but makes me happy:

- Tablet
- Video games
- Marshmallow-flavored lip gloss
- Art supplies

Stuff I would've been okay without:

- Pink bendy straw

Squishy penguin toy

Plastic pudding cup
- Disposable water bottle

When it comes to stuff you need or don't need, focus on *you*. For one girl, a squishy, penguin-shaped fidget toy that lights up when you squeeze it might be fun for a few days but then end up in the trash. For another kid, like a girl with autism who has trouble focusing, that toy might be the most important thing to get her through the day.

Shop Smart

When you or your family buys things, you can choose companies that do their part to protect the environment. Look for products that . . .

- use as little packaging as possible, especially plastic. Most packaging ends up in the garbage.

- explain how the company uses earth-friendly practices. If a business really cares about the earth, it will give you specific details about what it's doing to help.

- come from your state. Transporting products and food across the country and the world uses a lot of fossil fuels, so buying things made nearby is usually better.

- will last a long time. Some products don't cost much money, but they break soon after you start using them. That means they end up in the garbage, and you have to buy something new.

It's hard to make earth-friendly choices at the store. Often, products that are good for the environment are more expensive or harder to And sometimes companies design their produ to look like they're good for the environment if they're not. This is called *greenwashing*.

Can You Spot Greenwashing?

Can you spot which of these products are disguised as earth-friendly (greenwashed), and which are actually good for the environment (true green)?

- A plastic bottle of water with a picture of a mountain on it.

  Greenwashed

  True green

- A shoe company that claims to plant a tree for every pair you buy. On its website, you can't find information about the company's use of earth-friendly materials or how many trees it's planted.

  Greenwashed

  True green

- A fast-food meal that comes with a plastic endangered animal toy. The bag is stamped with the logo of a well-known wildlife organization.

  Greenwashed

  True green

4. A local shop that lets you bring in your own containers to buy foods like flour and dried fruit. Each food has a label that says where in your state it comes from.

   Greenwashed

   True green

5. A fossil fuel company that uses terms like *clean coal* or *clean-burning gas* on a TV ad.

   Greenwashed

   True green

6. A grocery store that starts printing green leaves on its plastic bags and hangs up a We Recycle Plastic Bags sign.

   Greenwashed

   True green

Answers

1. **Greenwashed.** Single-use plastic bottles are terrible for the environment because they use up a lot of resources and end up in the garbage right away. Reusable bottles and water filling stations are better.

2. **Greenwashed.** A true green company would give you as many details about its products as possible so you can be sure you're making an earth-friendly choice.

3. **Greenwashed.** Plastic toys and disposable packaging usually end up in the trash. You can check with the wildlife organization to see if the restaurant simply donated money to use the logo, or if the organization is helping the restaurant become more earth friendly.

4. **True green.** This store makes it easy for people to shop without taking home extra packaging that ends up in the trash. It's also up-front about where its products come from, so you can be sure less gas was used to transport them.

5. **Greenwashed.** Even though some fossil fuels pollute more or less than others, they are never good for the environment.

6. **Greenwashed.** Plastic bags are very hard to recycle, and it's better if people don't use them in the first place. Instead, the store could encourage shoppers to bring reusable cloth bags from home.

Companies use greenwashing to convince well-meaning people to buy their products. They also do it to distract people from the more important issue: that companies could stop climate change by using different materials, switching to clean energy, and making true green products. These companies want you to feel like climate change is your fault and that you could solve earth's problems just by switching which brand of margarine you buy. It's not, and you couldn't.

Between 1988 and today, over half of all greenhouse gas emissions in the world have come from just 25 companies—not individual people.

In your Earth-Lover's Notebook, make a list of the greenwashed items you see next time you go to the store. If those products were true green, what would they look like? If you were in charge of a company, how would you do things differently?

Eat Your Way to a Healthier Climate

Change the planet by changing what's on your plate.

very year, one-third of all greenhouse gases humans create comes
rom producing food. Here are two big ways Americans can do better:

at more veggies and less meat especially beef).

Raising cows for beef puts 20 times more greenhouse gases into the atmosphere than growing high-protein vegetables such as beans.

Cows need a lot of space, and 80 percent of deforestation in the Amazon rain forest happens to make room for raising them. A lot of those forests are taken illegally from Indigenous people—people who have lived in an area for thousands of years.

One cow can release up to 50 gallons of methane (a greenhouse gas) every day by *burping*!

buurrp...

Keep food out of the trash can.

- A third of all the world's food is wasted, much of it in factories and restaurants.

- Food waste contributes to climate change as much as all road transportation does.

- When you do throw away food, try composting it to make healthy food for gardens and houseplants!

Eating habits are hard to change. We like what we like! Fortunately, even small changes every now and then can help.

Easy Summer Rolls
You Need:

- When you have the choice, try to pick foods grown or made in your state. Local food requires fewer fossil fuels to travel from the farm to your grocery store.

- Check out a vegetarian cookbook from the library. Choose a yummy-looking recipe and ask permission to cook it for your family. Even going meat-free one day each week can help fight climate change.

locally grown!

Tiny Tree Tops

Dinosaur Tails

X-Ray Vision Sticks

- Fruits and veggies that wilt or turn mushy don't have to go in the garbage. Make them delicious again by adding them to sweet breads, smoothies, and sauces!

- Are your younger siblings picky eaters? One study found that inventing fun names for veggies made kids more likely to eat them.

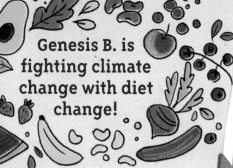

Genesis B. is fighting climate change with diet change!

Thirteen-year-old Genesis went vegan at age six because she wanted to protect animals. (A vegan is someone who doesn't eat meat or any product that comes from an animal, like milk or eggs.) But after some research, she learned that a veggie-based diet could protect the planet, too.

1300 Gallons = 1

First, she got her own family to stop eating animal products. Then she started giving speeches about fighting climate change with a vegan diet. "It takes up to 1,300 gallons of water just to produce one hamburger," she said in a TEDX speech when she was ten. "That's equivalent to almost two months of showers!"

Now she talks to friends, teachers, and leaders about how eating animals impacts the environment. She even challenged Pope Francis to go vegan! (He didn't, but her request convinced a lot of other people to eat less meat.) After she gets the world to go vegan, she hopes to become president of the United States.

"I have to make a difference today and I have to make a difference tomorrow. Because if I don't, we're just running out of time."
—Genesis B.

No Plastic? Fantastic.

Using less plastic is a great way to reduce your carbon footprint.

Plastic comes from fossil fuels. Companies extract oil from the ground, transport it to factories, power machines that refine it, and then power more machines that turn it into products and packaging. Every step of the way, greenhouse gases flow into the atmosphere.

9% Recycled

91% Garbage

- The United States recycles only 9 percent of its plastic. That means 91 percent of it piles up as garbage.

- 40 percent of plastic produced in the world is for packaging, like the bag that a loaf of bread comes in. Almost always, someone uses it once and then throws it away.

- Most plastic is so strong that it never goes away, it just keeps breaking up into smaller and smaller pieces that stay in the air or go into our water. These *microplastics* can get into our bodies when we breathe, drink water, or eat fish that have swallowed them.

- Eight million tons of plastic enters the oceans every year. Scientists estimate that at the rate we're going, there will be more plastic than fish in the oceans by 2050.

nowing the facts can make it easier to make smart choices throughout the day.

If you carry your lunch to school, use reusable containers instead of plastic bags, and avoid disposable packaging.

Say no to single-use plastic cups, forks, spoons, and straws whenever you can.

Carry a reusable water bottle.

Ready to think even **bigger?** Use the skills you learned in the Speaking Up for Solutions section to . . .

• help with a beach or river cleanup to keep plastic out of waterways.

• invent an alternative to your favorite plastic product that doesn't pollute the earth.

ask elected officials to restrict single-use plastics in your state.

educate the owner of your favorite café about how disposable cups and utensils affect the environment.

What other ideas do you have? Write them down in your Earth-Lover's Notebook.

Recycle

Turn your trash into something new!

The United States creates three times more trash than the average country—about 1,704 pounds of it every year, per person.

Average Country

That's like everyone throwing away four and a half soccer balls every day!

The best first step is not buying things like single-use plastics in the first place. But the best second step is recycling.

Here's how it works: You put a bottle, can, or piece of paper in a recycling bin. Someone takes the contents of that bin to a recycling center, sorts it into different categories, and sends each type of material to a special factory.

Metal is crushed into cubes, cut into tiny pieces, and melted back down into block shapes. From there, factories can use it to make other metal products, such as new cans or aluminum foil.

Plastic is shredded, melted, and shaped into tiny pellets. The pellets can be turned into new plastic containers and bottles, and even clothing.

Paper gets mixed with water until it turns into goop. Then a machine rolls it flat, lets it dry, and cuts it into new sheets of paper.

Create a recycling chart

It can be hard to remember which items go in the recycling bin and which don't. Make it easy for everyone with a recycling chart. Research the recycling rules for your town, write them down, and post them for everyone in your family to see.

RECYCLE

Plastic bottles and jugs (rinsed out, caps on)	
Glass jars and bottles (rinsed out)	
Metal cans (rinsed out)	
Paper and cardboard (flattened)	

1 PETE Polyethylene Terephthalate	2 HDPE High-Density Polyethylene	3 PVC Polyvinyl Chloride	4 LDPE Low-Density Polyethylene	5 PP Polypropylene	6 PS Polystyrene	7 OTHER Other
✓	✓	✗	✓	✓	✗	✗

Getting Around

Walking, biking, and riding public transportation are great ways to help the earth.

Every kid gets around a little differently. If you live in a big city, encourage your family to use the subway or bus.

About 15% of all greenhouse gases come from cars, trucks, trains, buses, and planes. We use more and more fossil fuels for transportation every year.

If you live in a town with sidewalks and bike trails, you might have fun walking or biking more often. In some towns, it's hard to go anywhere without a car, but you might be able to carpool with other families.

Fact: Most U.S. kids ride to school in cars, even when buses are available. Less than 15 percent of kids walk or ride a bike.

Write down the places you go most often (school, tae kwon do practice, your grandma Ethel's house) and how you get there (bus, bike, car, train):

I go to _____ by _____.

I go to _____ by _____.

I go to _____ by _____.

I go to _____ by _____.

Now put a check next to the trips you might be able to make more climate friendly by walking, biking, taking public transportation, or carpooling, even if it's just once in a while. And of course, always talk to your parents before changing how you get from place to place.

Ember and Azalea M. biked from New Hampshire to New York City!

It all started after seven-year-old Azalea watched a documentary about polar bears becoming endangered—she was so sad that she cried herself to sleep. The next morning, she and her nine-year-old sister Ember decided they had to do something to stop climate change.

With their mom, the girls set off on a bike trip from New Hampshire to New York City, where the 2019 UN Climate Action Summit was about to take place. Along the 200-mile trip, they raised about $800 for solar panels at their school. When pedaling got hard, Ember and Azalea thought about the polar bears suffering in the Arctic, and that gave them the strength to keep going.

It took sixteen days of biking, camping, and taking public transit when the roads got too dangerous. "We made it because we had passion," Azalea says. Ember adds, "We were passionate enough to not let the whole world burn on fire and melt."

The sisters are still raising money through their group, Kids Care 4 Polar Bears. They also work on environmental projects, like improving recycling at their school and talking to elected leaders about clean energy laws.

Be Kind

When you're devoted to a climate-friendly life, it's easy to point the finger at people who don't seem to care.

But it's *never* okay to shame someone for their own daily choices.

Climate change action looks different for everyone. For people with certain disabilities, using a straw might be the only way they can drink. For families who live on busy streets without sidewalks, walking or riding a bike to school might be too dangerous. And if a student gets lunch from school, they usually have no choice but to eat what the cafeteria serves. There are a million reasons why someone might not be able to make a climate-friendly choice.

Focus on the positive changes *you* can make. If you're tempted to call someone out for a choice you don't like, try these ideas instead:

- Ask your school cafeteria and local restaurants to consider switching to paper straws, or only giving out straws if people ask for them.

- Write a letter to your city council about creating more bike lanes so that more kids could bike around town safely. If you live in a rural area, ask your parents about starting a car pool with other kids.

- Do a school project about how producing meat contributes to climate change. During your presentation, bring in your favorite plant-based snack to share with the class.

Love the Earth, Love Yourself

When climate change gets too scary, it's time to take care of YOU.

Sometimes it can feel like climate change is happening too fast or that it's too late fix the problem. It can be especially tough if you're already struggling with the effects of climate change, like if pollution makes your asthma flare up, or if a flood has hurt your town. It's okay to feel discouraged or sad. Every activist does at one time or another.

Here are some ways to feel better:

- Talk to a parent about how you're feeling.

- Listen to your favorite music or watch your favorite movie.

- Chat with a friend who cares about climate change, too.

- Go for a walk. If you live near a hiking trail, spend some time among the trees to calm down.

Play your favorite sport, dance, or do cartwheels.

• Sit in a comfortable place and take slow, deep breaths. With each breath, think of something beautiful for each color of the rainbow.

Cuddle a pet.

• Imagine a world without climate change. Draw a picture of what it would look like, or write a story about it.

• If the bad feelings don't go away, ask an adult about going to a counselor or doctor for extra help.

For many activists, anger and sadness inspire them to take action. Years before starting her famous school strikes, Greta T. became so depressed about climate change that she couldn't talk, or even eat. Taking action and speaking out became her way to feel better.

On Your Mark, Get Set . . . Conserve!

Making earth-friendly choices works best when you love doing it. Try these challenges with your friends and family to make your activism fun!

Fashion face-off

Visit a secondhand shop with a friend. Each of you creates an outfit using only clothes and accessories you find there. Whoever comes up with the most stylish outfit wins!

> The fashion industry produces 10% of all greenhouse gas emissions.

Flair for repair

Find something at home that's broken, like a crackly speaker, a wobbly chair, or a pair of flip-flops. Instead of throwing it away, challenge yourself to fix it! Ask parent to help you look up videos onlin of people repairing similar things.

Gourmet grub game

Choose a food that you can normally only buy prepackaged at the store, like your favorite snack cake or chip. With a parent's help, see if you can re-create it in your own kitchen.

It takes a lot of fossil fuels to make processed snacks and the packages they come in. Together, food and packaging make up almost 45% of all waste in landfills.

Celebration challenge

Instead of buying single-use party decorations like balloons or plastic streamers, make your own! Start with cereal boxes, plastic bottles, and other items from your recycling bin, and see what you can create.

Farmers market madness

Play this game with your family if your community has a farmers market. Browse the market and pick out some fresh ingredients together. At home, work together to create a meal using only those ingredients!

Single-use plastics are filling up the ocean. In fact, 9 out of 10 ocean birds have plastic in their stomachs.

Food travels about 1,500 miles to reach most grocery stores, which puts a lot of greenhouse gases into the atmosphere. Food at farmers markets usually travels less than 200 miles.

Celebrate Your Love for the Earth

Loving the earth is something to celebrate! Here are ideas for a Love the Earth party you can throw any day of the year.

Snack: Veggie Chips

This snack is healthy for you and the earth! If you're up for it, look for the ingredients at a farmers market or community garden.

You will need:

- An adult to help you
- 6 kale leaves
- 2 red or yellow potatoes
- 2 sweet potatoes
- 4 tablespoons olive oil
- 1 teaspoon kosher salt
- 1 teaspoon ground black pepper

1. Preheat the oven to 350 degrees. Wash the kale and potatoes.

2. Pull the kale leaves off their hard stems. Tear the leaves into 2-inch pieces. Then, with an adult's help, cut the potatoes into thin slices.

3. Put the kale in one bowl and the potatoes in another bowl. Drizzle 2 tablespoons olive oil in each bowl. Add ½ teaspoon salt and ½ teaspoon pepper to each bowl. Mix well, until all the veggies are coated.

4. Arrange the kale on one baking sheet and the potatoes on another. Bake for 12 minutes. Take the kale out—it's done. Ask an adult to flip the potato slices and bake another 8 minutes.

5. Let the chips cool, mix them together, and then serve!

Be sure to use reusable plates and silverware for your guests!

Craft: Recycled T-shirt Bags

Making this craft is an easy way to recycle something old and create a great reusable bag. Before the party, ask your guests to bring some old T-shirts that they don't wear anymore. You can also check a thrift shop ahead of time to buy extras.

You will need:

- An old T-shirt
- Fabric scissors
- Marker
- Decorations like fabric markers, puff paint, and buttons (optional)

1. If your shirt has a design on it, decide whether you want it to face out. If so, turn it inside out. (When you're done, the pattern will face out.) If you're using an ugly shirt that your dad hasn't worn since 1999, keep it right-side out. (When you're done, the design will be hidden inside.)

2.

Lay the T-shirt flat and cut off both sleeves.

3.

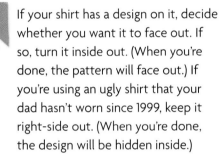

With a marker, draw a U shape below the collar. Then cut along the line to make the opening for your bag.

4.

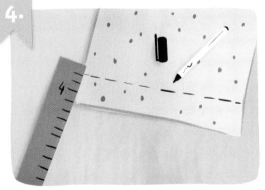

Use a ruler to draw a straight line about 4 inches from the bottom of the shirt.

5.

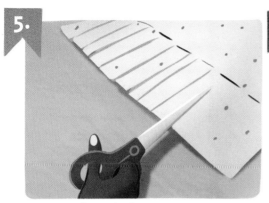

Cut strips from the bottom of the shirt to the line, about 1 inch apart.

6.

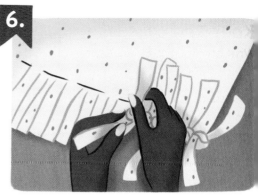

Tie each pair of strips together in a single knot

7.

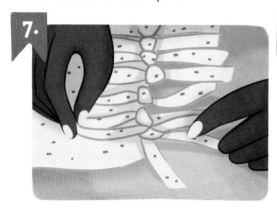

Now tie a second set of knots. This time, tie one strip from the first knot and one strip from the second knot together. Repeat all the way across. This helps fill in holes at the bottom of the bag.

8.

Turn the bag inside out. If you want to jazz it up, add decorations!

Keep the party going

What other activities would get your friends excited about loving the earth?

- **Fighting through writing.** Provide paper, pens, envelopes, and stamps. Have everyone write a letter to a politician or company that you think should work harder to stop climate change. Check out page 39 for an example letter.

- **Flower power.** Before the party, collect milk cartons from school and wash them. At the party, provide potting soil, flower seeds, and decorating supplies, like craft paint and stickers. Let each guest decorate her flower box and then plant a seed inside! Your friends will remember your party every time they check on their growing seed.

- **Relaxation station.** Mix oats, honey, and warm water to create an earth-friendly face mask. Let each guest spread some on her face and let it sit for 5–10 minutes. Then rinse it off and feel an earth-healthy glow!

Sanika knows how to party with purpose!

Twelve-year-old Sanika D. celebrated Earth Day by teaching preschoolers in her neighborhood about loving the earth. First, she showed the kids how to make eco-friendly chalk from cornstarch and water, and they made art on the sidewalk. Then she took them to the park for a recycling scavenger hunt and taught them how to recycle the items they found. They also read a book together about caring for the earth.

Fun without Fossil Fuels

There are so many ways to show your love for the earth. Here are some ideas to get started!

- Pick up trash and recyclables at a playground.

- Share a climate change article with your family.

- Bake homemade bread for a neighbor.

- Write an encouraging note to another climate change activist.

- Plant vegetables or flowers on your windowsill.

- Shovel a driveway instead of using a snowblower.

- Join your school's climate change club.

- Carry a reusable water bottle.

- Plan a no-meat day once a week. Try out new vegetarian or vegan recipes.

- Give a presentation to your class about an earth issue you care about.

- Listen to someone who's upset about climate change.

- Wear used clothing instead of buying it new.

- If you're able, bike or walk instead of riding in a car.

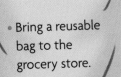

- Bring a reusable bag to the grocery store.

- Make your own wrapping paper out of paper bags or newspaper.

Community caring

- Attend a neighborhood meeting to talk about a climate change issue in your community.

- Make a homemade meal for a family going through a difficult time.

- Write a thank-you note to someone who's doing work for the earth.

- Ask a grocery store owner to let shoppers bring their own reusable containers for bulk foods like flour, oats, and dried fruit.

- Plant a tree.

- Buy fruits and veggies at a local farmers market.

- Hold a yard sale with friends and donate the proceeds to an earth-friendly charity.

- Read a book about climate change to kids at the library.

- Write a letter to the city council about a climate issue in your town.

- Ask a parent if you can pick up litter on a nearby hiking trail.

Make a poster about climate change and ask for permission to put it up at school.

- Watch a documentary about people around the world affected by climate change.

- Write a letter to a company that disappointed you by hurting the planet. Explain why you're not going to buy or use the company's products and what you'd like the company to change.

- Sell bracelets at school and donate your earnings to a worldwide organization you love.

- With a parent's permission, start a blog or video series about climate change.

- Create a video about greenwashed products you find at the store. Ask a parent to share it online to educate others.

- Write a letter to the president about an issue that worries you.

- Attend a climate change march.

Take the First Step

You love the earth. You have everything you need to change it for the better. And you can start *right now*.

What will you do first?

Here are some other American Girl books you might like:

Write to us!

Send your earth-lover stories to:

Love the Earth Editor
American Girl
8400 Fairway Place
Middleton, WI 53562

All comments and suggestions received by American Girl may be used without compensation or acknowledgment. We're sorry—photos can't be returned.